KING MIDAS

Retold by Catherine Storr

Illustrated by Mike Codd

Raintree Childrens Books
Milwaukee·Toronto·Melbourne·London
Belitha Press Limited·London

Copyright © in this format Belitha Press Ltd., 1985

Text copyright © Catherine Storr 1985

Illustrations copyright © Mike Codd 1985

Art Director: Treld Bicknell

First published in the United States of America 1985
by Raintree Publishers Inc.
330 East Kilbourn Avenue, Milwaukee, Wisconsin 53202
in association with Belitha Press Ltd., London.

Library of Congress Number: 84-18307

Conceived, designed and produced by Belitha Press Ltd.,
2 Beresford Terrace, London N5 2DH

ISBN 0-8172-2112-3 (U.S.A.)

Library of Congress Cataloging in Publication Data

Storr, Catherine
  King Midas

  (Raintree stories)
  (Summary: A king who wishes for the golden touch is faced with its
unfortunate consequences.
  1. Midas—Juvenile literature. [1. Midas. 2. Mythology, Greek]
I. Codd, Michael, ill. II. Title.
BL820.M55S76   1985   398.2′2   84-18307
ISBN 0-8172-2112-3

First published in Great Britain 1985
by Methuen Children's Books Ltd.,
11 New Fetter Lane, London EC4P 4EE

1 2 3 4 5 6 7 8 9   89   88   87   86   85

Note: The source for the story is *The Greek Myths* by Robert Graves.

C.S.

Printed in Hong Kong by South China Printing Co.

Once upon a time there was a king called Midas.
He was very rich. He lived in a marble palace
decorated with gold. He had a golden throne to sit on
and a golden crown to wear on his head.

King Midas had chests full of treasures—golden necklaces, golden bracelets, and golden rings. Inside his palace he had trees made by clever craftsmen, with gold and silver leaves. The fruit that hung from the branches was made of precious jewels—emerald and ruby, amethyst and topaz and lapis lazuli.

One day, the men who worked in Midas' garden found an old, shabby man asleep among the rose bushes. They tied his hands and feet with garlands of roses, and carried him to King Midas as their prisoner.

"Who are you? And what are you doing in my garden?" Midas asked the man.

"Great King, the god of wine, Dionysus, has many followers. I am one of them. I am old Silenus. If you will set me free so that I can join him again, I will tell you the most wonderful stories that you have ever heard."

Midas kept Silenus in his palace for five days and nights, and he listened to his stories.

"I will tell you," said Silenus, "how there is a great land, far away beyond the sea. It is full of splendid cities, and the people who live there are happy and tall, and they live nearly forever.

"Or shall I tell you about the terrible whirlpool which no human has ever been able to cross?

Nearby are two streams, and on the banks of the
streams grow two different kinds of tree. The man
who eats the fruit of the first kind becomes miserable,
and he cries and groans until he dies. The man who
eats the fruit of the second kind of tree grows younger
every day. Even old men can become babies again."

After hearing these stories, Midas let Silenus go. The god Dionysus sent a message to Midas. "I will reward you for looking after my old friend. Tell me what your dearest wish is, and I will grant it."

Midas said at once, "I should like best that everything I touch should turn into gold."

"**T**hink carefully about what you are asking for,"
Dionysus said. But Midas would not stop to
think. He wanted to be the richest man in the world.
Dionysus said, "Then I will grant your wish.
From now on, you have the Golden Touch."

Midas was delighted. He touched the stone bench in the garden. It immediately turned into gold. He picked up a pebble from the ground and found that he held a nugget of gold.

"Wonderful! I shall have a golden palace! I will have a forest of golden trees! Everything around me will be made of gold!" Midas said. He went around his palace and his garden, turning stone and wood and marble into gold. The roses now had heavy golden blossoms and leaves, on golden stems stiff with golden thorns.

Presently Midas was hungry and thirsty. He went into his palace and sat at his table. He called to his servants to bring him a cup of wine. Midas was delighted when he saw that as his fingers touched the cup, it turned into a golden goblet.

B ut as his tongue tasted the wine, that, too, turned into solid gold.

"Bring me food!" he commanded. His cooks brought their choicest dishes and set them before him. But when the meat and the bread reached his mouth, they became gold, as hard as stone. He took a peach from the golden salver, and it lay heavy and cold in his hand.

"Alas! I have been a fool! I have asked for the Golden Touch, and now, even though I am the richest man in the world, I must die of hunger and thirst!" said Midas.

He called out to the god, Dionysus. He said, "Great god! You were right, and I was wrong. Forgive me! Take back your gift!"

Dionysus laughed. But he was sorry for King Midas. He told him, "Go and wash in the river, and you will be free from the Golden Touch. Then everything that has changed will become itself again."

The trees swayed in the wind. The flowers smelled sweet. Midas ate a huge meal. He enjoyed the red wine and the good bread.

He was very happy now, even though he was no longer the richest man in the world.